THE OPEN MEDIA PAMPHLET SERIES

OTHER OPEN MEDIA PAMPHLET SERIES TITLES

OPEN MEDIA BOOKS

THE OPEN MEDIA PAMPHLET SERIES

ACTS OF AGGRESSION

POLICING "ROGUE STATES"

NOAM CHOMSKY

WITH EDWARD W. SAID

Series editor Greg Ruggiero

SEVEN STORIES PRESS / New York

ISBN: 1-58322-546-3

Cover photo: A Tomahawk cruise missile launches
from the forward vertical launch system of the
U.S.S. Shiloh to attack points in the 33rd parallel
in Iraq on Sept. 3, 1996, as part of Operation
Desert Strike. U.S. DEPARTMENT OF DEFENSE

Book design by Cindy LaBreacht

9 8 7 6 5 4

Printed in Canada.

CONTENTS

APOCALYPSE NOW

by Edward W. Said

First published in Arabic in *Al-Hayat*, London, and in English in *Al Ahram Weekly*, Cairo.

It would be a mistake, I think, to reduce what is happening between Iraq and the United States simply to an assertion of Arab will and sovereignty versus American imperialism, which undoubtedly plays a central role in all this. However misguided, Saddam Hussein's cleverness is not that he is splitting America from its allies (which he has not really succeeded in doing for any practical purpose) but that he is exploiting the astonishing clumsiness and failures of U.S. foreign policy. Very few people, least of all Saddam himself, can be fooled into believing him to be the innocent victim of American bullying; most of what is happening to his unfortunate people who are undergoing the most dreadful and unacknowledged suffering is due in considerable degree to his callous cynicism—first of all, his indefensible and ruinous invasion of Kuwait, his persecution of the Kurds, his cruel egoism and pompous self-regard which persists in aggrandizing himself and his regime at exorbitant and, in my opinion, totally unwarranted cost. It is impossible for him to plead the case for national security and sovereignty given his abysmal disregard of it in the case of Kuwait and Iran. Be that as it may, U.S. vindictiveness, whose sources I shall look at in a moment, has exacerbated the situation by imposing a regime of sanctions which, as Sandy Berger, the American national security adviser has proudly said, is unprecedented for its severity in the whole of world history. It is believed that 567,000 Iraqi civilians have died since the Gulf War, mostly as a result of disease, malnutrition and deplorably poor medical care. Agriculture and industry are at a total standstill. This is unconscionable of course, and for this the brazen inhumanity of American policy-makers is also very largely to blame. But we must not forget that Saddam is feeding that inhumanity quite deliberately in order to dramatize the opposition between the United States and the rest of the Arab world; having provoked a crisis with the United States (or the United Nations dominated by the United States) he at first dramatized the unfairness of the sanctions. But by continuing it, the issue has changed and has become his non-compliance, and the terrible effects of the sanctions have been marginalized. Still the underlying causes of an Arab/U.S. crisis remain. A careful analysis of that crisis is imperative. The United States has always opposed any sign of Arab nationalism or independence, partly for its own imperial reasons and partly because its unconditional support for Israel requires it to do so. Since the 1973 war, and despite the brief oil embargo, Arab policy up to and including the peace process has tried to circumvent or mitigate that hostility by appealing to the United States for help, by "good" behavior, by willingness to make peace with Israel. Yet mere compliance with the wishes of the United States can produce nothing except occasional words of American approbation for leaders who appear "moderate": Arab policy was never backed up with coordination, or collective pressure, or fully agreed upon goals. Instead each leader tried to make separate arrangements both with the United States and with Israel, none of which produced very much except escalating demands and a constant refusal by the United States to exert any meaningful pressure on Israel. The more extreme Israeli policy becomes the more likely the United States has been to support it. And the less respect it has for the large mass of Arab peoples whose future and well-being are mortgaged to illusory hopes embodied, for instance, in the Oslo accords.

Moreover, a deep gulf separates Arab culture and civilization from the United States, and in the absence of any collective Arab information and cultural policy, the notion of an Arab people with traditions, cultures and identities of their own is

8

simply inadmissible in the United States. Arabs are dehumanized, they are seen as violent irrational terrorists always on the lookout for murder and bombing outrages. The only Arabs worth doing business with for the United States are compliant leaders, businessmen, and military people whose arms purchases (the highest per capita in the world) are helping the American economy keep afloat. Beyond that there is no feeling at all, for instance, for the dreadful suffering of the Iraqi people whose identity and existence have simply been lost sight of in the present situation. This morbid, obsessional fear and hatred of the Arabs has been a constant theme in U.S. foreign policy since World War Two. In some way also, anything positive about the Arabs is seen in the United States as a threat to Israel. In this respect pro-Israeli American Jews, traditional Orientalists, and military hawks have played a devastating role. Moral opprobrium is heaped on Arab states as it is on no others. Turkey, for example, has been conducting a campaign against the Kurds for several years, yet nothing is heard about this in the United States. Israel occupies territory illegally for thirty years, it violates the Geneva conventions at will, conducts invasions, terrorist attacks and assassinations against Arabs, and still, the United States vetoes every sanction against it in the United Nations. Syria, Sudan, Libya, Iraq are classified as "rogue" states. Sanctions against them are far harsher than against any other countries in the history of U.S. foreign policy. And still the United States expects that its own foreign policy agenda ought to prevail (e.g., the woefully misguided Doha economic summit) despite its hostility to the collective Arab agenda. In the case of Iraq a number of further extenuations make the United States even more repressive. Burning in the collective American unconscious is a puritanical zeal decreeing the sternest possible attitude towards anyone deemed to be an unregenerate sinner. This clearly guided American policy towards the native American Indians, who were first demonized, then portrayed as wasteful savages, then exterminated, their tiny remnant confined to reservations and concentration camps. This almost religious anger fuels a judgemental attitude that has no place at all in international politics, but for the United States it is a central tenet of its worldwide behavior. Second, punishment is conceived in apocalyptic terms. During the Vietnam war a leading general advocated—and almost achieved—the goal of bombing the enemy into the stone age. The same view prevailed during the Gulf War in 1991. Sinners are meant to be condemned terminally, with the utmost cruelty regardless of whether or not they suffer the cruelest agonies. The notion of "justified" punishment for Iraq is now uppermost in the minds of most American consumers of news, and with that goes an almost orgiastic delight in the power used to confront Iraq in the Gulf.

Pictures of immense U.S. warships steaming virtuously away punctuate breathless news bulletins about Saddam's defiance, and the impending crisis. President Clinton announces that he is thinking not about the Gulf but about the 21st century: how can we tolerate Iraq's threat to use biological warfare even though (this is unmentioned) it is clear from the United Nations Special Committee (UNSCOM) reports that he neither has the missile capacity, nor the chemical arms, nor the nuclear arsenal, nor in fact the anthrax bombs that he is alleged to be brandishing? Forgotten in all this is that the United States has all the terror weapons known to humankind, is the only country to have used a nuclear bomb on civilians, and as recently as seven years ago dropped 66,000 tons of bombs on Iraq. As the only country involved in this crisis that has never had to fight a war on its own soil, it is easy for the United States and its mostly brain-washed citizens to speak in apocalyptic terms. A report out of Australia on Sunday, November 16 suggests that Israel and the United States are thinking about a neutron bomb on Baghdad. Unfortunately the dictates of raw power are very severe and, for a weak state like Iraq, overwhelming. Certainly U.S. misuse of the sanctions to strip Iraq of everything, including any possibility for security is monstrously sadistic. The so-called U.N. 661 Committee created to oversee the sanctions is composed of fifteen member states (including the United States) each of which has a veto. Every time Iraq passes this committee a request to sell oil for medicines, trucks, meat, etc., any member of the committee can block these requests by saying that a given item may have military purposes (tires, for example, or ambulances). In addition, the United States and its clients—e.g., the unpleasant and racist Richard Butler, who says openly that Arabs have a different notion of truth than the rest of the world—have made it clear that even if Iraq is completely reduced militarily to the point where it is no longer a threat to its neighbors (which is now the case) the real goal of the sanctions is to topple Saddam Hussein's government. According to the American government, very little that Iraq can do short of Saddam's resignation or death will produce a lifting of sanctions. Finally, we should not for a moment forget that quite apart from its foreign policy interest, Iraq has now become a domestic American issue whose repercussions on issues unrelated to oil or the Gulf are very important. Bill Clinton's personal crises—the campaign-funding scandals, an impending trial for sexual harassment, his various legislative and domestic failures—require him to look strong, determined

12

and "presidential" somewhere else, and where but in the Gulf against Iraq has he so ready-made a foreign devil to set off his blue-eyed strength to full advantage. Moreover, the increase in military expenditure for new investments in electronic "smart" weaponry, more sophisticated aircraft, mobile forces for the world-wide projection of American power are perfectly suited for display and use in the Gulf, where the likelihood of visible casualties (actually suffering Iraqi civilians) is extremely small, and where the new military technology can be put through its paces most attractively. For reasons that need restating here, the media is particularly happy to go along with the government in bringing home to domestic customers the wonderful excitement of American self-righteousness, the proud flag-waving, the "feel-good" sense that "we" are facing down a monstrous dictator. Far from analysis and calm reflection, the media exists mainly to derive its mission from the government, not to produce a corrective or any dissent. The media, in short, is an extension of the war against Iraq.

The saddest aspect of the whole thing is that Iraqi civilians seem condemned to additional suffering and protracted agony. Neither their government nor that of the United States is inclined to ease the daily pressure on them, and the probability that only they will pay for the crisis is extremely high. At least—and it isn't very much—there seems to be no enthusiasm among Arab governments for American military action, but beyond that there is no coordinated Arab position, not even on the extremely grave humanitarian question. It is unfortunate that, according to the news, there is rising popular support for Saddam in the Arab world, as if the old lessons of defiance without real power have still not been learned. Undoubtedly the United States has manipulated the United Nations to its own ends, a rather shameful exercise given at the same time that the Congress once again struck down a motion to pay a billion dollars in arrears to the world organization. The major priority for Arabs, Europeans, Muslims and Americans is to push to the fore the issue of sanctions and the terrible suffering imposed on innocent Iraqi civilians. Taking the case to the International Court in the Hague strikes me as a perfectly viable possibility, but what is needed is a concerted will on behalf of Arabs who have suffered the U.S.'s egregious blows for too long without an adequate response.

ROGUE STATES

by Noam Chomsky

First published in *Z* magazine, April 1998.

The concept of "rogue state" plays a pre-eminent role today in policy planning and analysis. The current Iraq crisis is only the latest example. Washington and London declared Iraq a "rogue state," a threat to its neighbors and to the entire world, an "outlaw nation" led by a reincarnation of Hitler who must be contained by the guardians of world order, the United States and its British "junior partner," to adopt the term ruefully employed by the British foreign office half a century ago. The concept merits a closer look. But first, let's consider its application in the current crisis.

The most interesting feature of the debate over the Iraq crisis is that it never took place. True, many words flowed, and there was dispute about how to proceed. But discussion kept within rigid bounds that excluded the obvious answer: the United States and Britain should act in accord with their laws and treaty obligations.

The relevant legal framework is formulated in the Charter of the United Nations, a "solemn treaty" recognized as the foundation of international law and world order, and under the U.S.

Constitution, "the supreme law of the land."

The Charter states that "The Security Council shall determine the existence of any threat to the peace, breach of the peace, or act of aggression, and shall make recommendations, or decide what measures shall be taken in accordance with Articles 41 and 42," which detail the preferred "measures not involving the use of armed force" and permit the Security Council to take further action if it finds such measures inadequate. The only exception is Article 51, which permits the "right of individual or collective self-defense" against "armed attack... until the Security Council has taken the measures necessary to maintain international peace and security." Apart from these exceptions, member states "shall refrain in their international relations from the threat or use of force."

There are legitimate ways to react to the many threats to world peace. If Iraq's neighbors feel threatened, they can approach the Security Council to authorize appropriate measures to respond to the threat. If the United States and Britain feel threatened, they can do the same. But no state has the authority to make its own determinations on these matters and to act as it chooses; the United States and Britain would have no such authority even if their own hands were clean, hardly the case.

Outlaw states do not accept these conditions:

Saddam's Iraq, for example, or the United States. Its position was forthrightly articulated by Secretary of State Madeleine Albright, then U.N. Ambassador, when she informed the Security Council during an earlier U.S. confrontation with Iraq that the United States will act "multilaterally when we can and unilaterally as we must," because "We recognize this area as vital to U.S. national interests" and therefore accept no external constraints. Albright reiterated that stand when U.N. Secretary-General Kofi Annan undertook his February 1998 diplomatic mission: "We wish him well," she stated, "and when he comes back we will see what he has brought and how it fits with our national interest," which will determine how we respond. When Annan announced that an agreement had been reached, Albright repeated the doctrine: "It is possible that he will come with something we don't like, in which case we will pursue our national interest." President Clinton announced that if Iraq fails the test of conformity (as determined by Washington), "everyone would understand that then the United States and hopefully all of our allies would have the unilateral right to respond at a time, place and manner of our own choosing," in the manner of other violent and lawless states.

The Security Council unanimously endorsed Annan's agreement, rejecting U.S./U.K. demands that it authorize their use of force in the event of non-compliance. The resolution warned of "severest consequences," but with no further specification. In the crucial final paragraph, the Council "decides, in accordance with its responsibilities under the Charter, to remain actively seized of the matter, in order to ensure implementation of this resolution and to ensure peace and security in the area." The Council, no one else; in accordance with the Charter.

The facts were clear and unambiguous. Headlines read: "An Automatic Strike Isn't Endorsed" (*Wall Street Journal*); "U.N. Rebuffs U.S. on Threat to Iraq if it Breaks Pact" (*New York Times*); etc. Britain's U.N. Ambassador "privately assured his colleagues on the Council that the resolution does not grant the United States and Britain an 'automatic trigger' to launch strikes against Iraq if it impedes" U.N. searches. "It has to be the Security Council who determines when to use armed force," the Ambassador of Costa Rica declared, expressing the position of the Security Council.

Washington's reaction was different. U.S. Ambassador Bill Richardson asserted that the agreement "did not preclude the unilateral use of force" and that the United States retains its legal right to attack Baghdad at will. State Department spokesperson James Rubin dismissed the wording of the resolution as "not as relevant as the kind of private discussions that we've had": "I am not saying that we don't care about that resolution," but "we've made clear that we don't see the need to return to the Security Council if there is a violation of the agreement." The President stated that the resolution "provides authority to act" if the United States is dissatisfied with Iraqi compliance; his press secretary made clear that that means military action. "U.S. Insists It Retains Right to Punish Iraq," the *New York Times* headline read, accurately. The United States has the unilateral right to use force at will: Period.

Some felt that even this stand strayed too close to our solemn obligations under international and domestic law. Senate majority leader Trent Lott denounced the Administration for having "subcontracted" its foreign policy "to others"—to the U.N. Security Council. Senator John McCain warned that "the United States may be subordinating its power to the United Nations," an obligation only for law-abiding states. Senator John Kerry added that it would be "legitimate" for the United States to invade Iraq outright if Saddam "remains obdurate and in violation of the United Nations resolutions, and in a position of threat to the world community," whether the Security Council so determines or not. Such unilateral U.S. action would be "within the framework of international law," as Kerry conceives it. A liberal dove who reached national prominence as an opponent of the Vietnam War, Kerry explained that his current stand was consistent with his earlier views. Vietnam taught him that the force should be used only if the objective is "achievable and it meets the needs of your country." Saddam's invasion of Kuwait was therefore wrong for only one reason: it was not "achievable," as matters turned out.

At the liberal-dovish end of the spectrum, Annan's agreement was welcomed, but within the narrow framework that barred the central issues. In a typical reaction, the *Boston Globe* stated that had Saddam not backed down, "the United States would not only have been justified in attacking Iraq—it would have been irresponsible not to," with no further questions asked. The editors also called for "a universal consensus of opproprium" against "weapons of mass destruction" as "the best chance the world has of keeping perverted science from inflicting hitherto unimagined harm." A sensible proposal; one can think of easy ways to start, without the threat of force, but these are not what are intended.

Political analyst William Pfaff deplored Washington's unwillingness to consult "theological or philosophical opinion," the views of Thomas Aquinas and Renaissance theologian Francisco Suarez—as "a part of the analytical community" in the United States and Britain had done "during the 1950s and 1960s," seeking guidance from "philosophy and theology"! But not the foundations of contemporary international and domestic law, which are explicit, though irrelevant to the intellectual culture. Another liberal analyst urged the United States to face the fact that if its incomparable power "is really being exercised for mankind's sake, mankind demands some say in its use," which would not be permitted by "the Constitution, the Congress nor television's Sunday pundits"; "And the other nations of the world have not assigned Washington the right to decide when, where and how their interests should be served" (Ronald Steel).

The Constitution does happen to provide such mechanisms, namely, by declaring valid treaties "the supreme law of the land," particularly the most fundamental of them, the U.N. Charter. It further authorizes Congress to "define and punish... offenses against the law of nations," undergirded by the Charter in the contemporary era. It is, furthermore, a bit of an understatement to say that other nations "have not assigned Washington the right"; they have forcefully denied it that right, following the (at least rhetorical) lead of Washington, which largely crafted the Charter.

Reference to Iraq's violation of U.N. resolutions was regularly taken to imply that the two warrior states have the right to use force unilaterally, taking the role of "world policemen"—an insult to the police, who in principle are supposed to enforce the law, not tear it to shreds. There was criticism of Washington's "arrogance of power," and the like, not quite the proper terms for a self-designated violent outlaw state.

One might contrive a tortured legal argument to support U.S./U.K. claims, though no one really tried. Step one would be that Iraq has violated U.N. Resolution 687 of April 3, 1991, which declares a cease-fire "upon official notification by Iraq" that it accepts the provisions that are spelled out (destruction of weapons, inspection, etc.). This is probably the longest and most detailed Security Council Resolution on record, but it mentions no enforcement mechanism. Step two of the argument, then, would be that Iraq's non-compliance "reinvokes" Resolution 678 (November 29, 1990). That Resolution authorizes member states "to use all necessary means to uphold and implement Resolution 660" (August 2, 1990), which calls on Iraq to withdraw at once from Kuwait and for Iraq and Kuwait "to begin immediately intensive negotiations for the resolution of their differences," recommending the framework of the Arab League. Resolution 678 also invokes "all subsequent relevant resolutions" (listing them: 662, 664); these are "relevant" in that they refer to the occupation of Kuwait and Iraqi actions relating to it. Reinvoking 678 thus leaves matters as they were: with no authorization to use force to implement the later Resolution 687, which brings up completely different issues, authorizing nothing beyond sanctions.

There is no need to debate the matter. The United States and Britain could readily have settled all doubts by calling on the Security Council to authorize their "threat and use of force," as required by the Charter. Britain did take some steps in that direction, but abandoned them when it became obvious, at once, that the Security Council would not go along. But these considerations have little relevance in a world dominated by rogue states that reject the rule of law.

Suppose that the Security Council were to authorize the use of force to punish Iraq for violating the cease-fire U.N. Resolution 687. That authorization would apply to all states: for example, to Iran, which would therefore be entitled to invade southern Iraq to sponsor a rebellion. Iran is a neighbor and the victim of U.S.-backed Iraqi aggression and chemical warfare, and could claim, not implausibly, that its invasion would have some local support; the United States and Britain can make no such claim. Such Iranian actions, if imaginable, would never be tolerated, but would be far less outrageous than the plans of the self-appointed enforcers. It is hard to imagine such elementary observations entering public discussion in the United States and Britain.

Contempt for the rule of law is deeply rooted in U.S. practice and intellectual culture. Recall, for example, the reaction to the judgment of the World

Court in 1986 condemning the United States for "unlawful use of force" against Nicaragua, demanding that it desist and pay extensive reparations, and declaring all U.S. aid to the contras, whatever its character, to be "military aid," not "humanitarian aid." The Court was denounced on all sides for having discredited itself. The terms of the judgment were not considered fit to print, and were ignored. The Democrat-controlled Congress immediately authorized new funds to step up the unlawful use of force. Washington vetoed a Security Council resolution calling on all states to respect international law—not mentioning anyone, though the intent was clear.

When the General Assembly passed a similar resolution, the United States voted against it, effectively vetoing it, joined only by Israel and El Salvador; the following year, only the automatic Israeli vote could be garnered. Little of this received mention in the media or journals of opinion, let alone what it signifies.

Secretary of State George Shultz meanwhile explained (April 14, 1986) that "Negotiations are a euphemism for capitulation if the shadow of power is not cast across the bargaining table." He condemned those who advocate "utopian, legalistic means like outside mediation, the United Nations, and the World Court, while ignoring the power element of the equation"—sentiments not without precedent in modern history.

24

The open contempt for Article 51 is particularly revealing. It was demonstrated with remarkable clarity immediately after the 1954 Geneva accords on a peaceful settlement for Indochina, regarded as a "disaster" by Washington, which moved at once to undermine them. The National Security Council secretly decreed that even in the case of "local Communist subversion or rebellion *not constituting armed attack*," the United States would consider the use of military force, including an attack on China if it is "determined to be the source" of the "subversion" (NSC 5429/2; my emphasis). The wording, repeated verbatim annually in planning documents, was chosen so as to make explicit the U.S. right to violate Article 51. The same document called for remilitarizing Japan, converting Thailand into "the focal point of U.S. covert and psychological operations in Southeast Asia," undertaking "covert operations on a large and effective scale" throughout Indochina, and in general, acting forcefully to undermine the Accords and the U.N. Charter. This critically important document was grossly falsified by the *Pentagon Papers* historians, and has largely disappeared from history.

The United States proceeded to define "aggression" to include "political warfare, or subversion" (by someone else, that is)—what Adlai Stevenson called "internal aggression" while defending J.F.K.'s escalation to a full-scale attack against South Vietnam. When the United States bombed Libyan cities in 1986, the official justification was "self defense against future attack." *New York Times* legal specialist Anthony Lewis praised the Administration for relying "on a legal argument that violence [in this case] is justified as an act of self-defense," under this creative interpretation of Article 51 of the Charter, which would have embarrassed a literate high school student. The U.S. invasion of Panama was defended in the Security Council by Ambassador Thomas Pickering by appeal to Article 51, which, he declared, "provides for the use of armed force to defend a country, to defend our interests and our people," and entitles the United States to invade Panama to prevent its "territory from being used as a base for smuggling drugs into the United States." Educated opinion nodded sagely in assent.

In June 1993, Clinton ordered a missile attack on Iraq, killing civilians and greatly cheering the president, congressional doves, and the press, who found the attack "appropriate, reasonable and necessary." Commentators were particularly impressed by Ambassador Albright's appeal to Article 51. The bombing, she explained, was in "self-defense against armed attack"—namely, an alleged attempt to assassinate former president Bush two months earlier, an appeal that would have scarcely risen to the level of absurdity even if the United States had been able to demonstrate

Iraqi involvement; "Administration officials, speaking anonymously," informed the press "that the judgment of Iraq's guilt was based on circumstantial evidence and analysis rather than ironclad intelligence," the *New York Times* reported, dismissing the matter. The press assured elite opinion that the circumstances "plainly fit" Article 51 (*Washington Post*). "Any President has a duty to use military force to protect the nation's interests" (*New York Times*, while expressing some skepticism about the case in hand). "Diplomatically, this was the proper rationale to invoke," and "Clinton's reference to the U.N. charter conveyed an American desire to respect international law" (*Boston Globe*). Article 51 "permits states to respond militarily if they are threatened by a hostile power" (*Christian Science Monitor*). Article 51 entitles a state to use force "in self-defence against threats to one's nationals," British Foreign Secretary Douglas Hurd instructed Parliament, supporting Clinton's "justified and proportionate exercise of the right of self-defence." There would be a "dangerous state of paralysis" in the world, Hurd continued, if the United States were required to gain Security Council approval before launching missiles against an enemy that might—or might not—have ordered a failed attempt to kill an ex-President two months earlier.

The record lends considerable support to the concern widely voiced about "rogue states" that are dedicated to the rule of force, acting in the "national interest" as defined by domestic power; most ominously, rogue states that anoint themselves global judge and executioner.

ROGUE STATES: THE NARROW CONSTRUCTION

It is also interesting to review the issues that did enter the non-debate on the Iraq crisis. But first a word about the concept "rogue state."

The basic conception is that although the Cold War is over, the United States still has the responsibility to protect the world—but from what? Plainly it cannot be from the threat of "radical nationalism"—that is, unwillingness to submit to the will of the powerful. Such ideas are only fit for internal planning documents, not the general public. From the early 1980s, it was clear that the conventional technique for mass mobilization was losing its effectiveness: the appeal to J.F.K.'s "monolithic and ruthless conspiracy," Reagan's "evil empire." New enemies were needed.

At home, fear of crime—particularly drugs—was stimulated by "a variety of factors that have little or nothing to do with crime itself," the National Criminal Justice Commission concluded, including media practices and "the role of government and private industry in stoking citizen fear," "exploiting latent racial tension for political purposes," with racial bias in enforce-

NOAM CHOMSKY

ment and sentencing that is devastating black communities, creating a "racial abyss" and putting "the nation at risk of a social catastrophe." The results have been described by criminologists as "the American Gulag," "the new American Apartheid," with African Americans now a majority of prisoners for the first time in U.S. history, imprisoned at well over seven times the rate of whites, completely out of the range of arrest rates, which themselves target blacks far out of proportion to drug use or trafficking.

Abroad, the threats were to be "international terrorism," "Hispanic narcotraffickers," and most serious of all, "rogue states." A secret 1995 study of the Strategic Command, which is responsible for the strategic nuclear arsenal, outlines the basic thinking. Released through the Freedom of Information Act, the study, *Essentials of Post–Cold War Deterrence*, "shows how the United States shifted its deterrent strategy from the defunct Soviet Union to so-called rogue states such as Iraq, Libya, Cuba and North Korea," AP reports. The study advocates that the United States exploit its nuclear arsenal to portray itself as "irrational and vindictive if its vital interests are attacked." That "should be a part of the national persona we project to all adversaries," particularly the "rogue states." "It hurts to portray ourselves as too fully rational and cool-headed," let alone committed to such silliness as international law and treaty obligations. "The fact that some elements" of the U.S. government "may appear to be potentially 'out of control' can be beneficial to creating and reinforcing fears and doubts within the minds of an adversary's decision makers." The report resurrects Nixon's "madman theory": our enemies should recognize that we are crazed and unpredictable, with extraordinary destructive force at our command, so they will bend to our will in fear. The concept was apparently devised in Israel in the 1950s by the governing Labor Party, whose leaders "preached in favor of acts of madness," Prime Minister Moshe Sharett records in his diary, warning that "we will go crazy" ("nishtagea") if crossed, a "secret weapon" aimed in part against the United States, not considered sufficiently reliable at the time. In the hands of the world's sole superpower, which regards itself as an outlaw state and is subject to few constraints from elites within, that stance poses no small problem for the world.

Libya was a favorite choice as "rogue state" from the earliest days of the Reagan administration. Vulnerable and defenseless, it is a perfect punching bag when needed: for example, in 1986, when the first bombing in history orchestrated for prime time TV was used by the Great Communicator's speech writers to muster support for Washington's terrorist forces attacking Nicaragua, on grounds that the "archterrorist"

Qaddafi "has sent $400 million and an arsenal of weapons and advisors into Nicaragua to bring his war home to the United States," which was then exercising its right of self-defense against the armed attack of the Nicaraguan rogue state.

Immediately after the Berlin Wall fell, ending any resort to the Soviet threat, the Bush administration submitted its annual call to Congress for a huge Pentagon budget. It explained that "In a new era, we foresee that our military power will remain an essential underpinning of the global balance, but... the more likely demands for the use of our military forces may not involve the Soviet Union and may be in the Third World, where new capabilities and approaches may be required," as "when President Reagan directed American naval and air forces to return to [Libya] in 1986" to bombard civilian urban targets, guided by the goal of "contributing to an international environment of peace, freedom and progress within which our democracy—and other free nations—can flourish." The primary threat we face is the "growing technological sophistication" of the Third World. We must therefore strengthen "the defense industrial base"—a.k.a. high tech industry—creating incentives "to invest in new facilities and equipment as well as in research and development." And we must maintain intervention forces, particularly those targeting the Middle East, where the "threats to our interests" that have required direct military engagement "could not be laid at the Kremlin's door" —contrary to endless fabrication, now put to rest. As had occasionally been recognized in earlier years, sometimes in secret, the "threat" is now conceded officially to be indigenous to the region, the "radical nationalism" that has always been a primary concern, not only in the Middle East.

At the time, the "threats to our interests" could not be laid at Iraq's door either. Saddam was then a favored friend and trading partner. His status changed only a few months later, when he misinterpreted U.S. willingness to allow him to modify the border with Kuwait by force as authorization to take the country over—or from the perspective of the Bush administration, to duplicate what the United States had just done in Panama. At a high-level meeting immediately after Saddam's invasion of Kuwait, President Bush articulated the basic problem: "My worry about the Saudis is that they're... going to bug out at the last minute and accept a puppet regime in Kuwait." Chair of the Joint Chiefs Colin Powell posed the problem sharply: "The next few days Iraq will withdraw," putting "his puppet in" and "Everyone in the Arab world will be happy."

Historical parallels are never exact, of course. When Washington partially withdrew from Panama after putting its puppet in, there was great anger throughout the hemisphere, including Panama. Indeed throughout much of the world, compelling Washington to veto two Security Council resolutions and to vote against a General Assembly resolution condemning Washington's "flagrant violation of international law and of the independence, sovereignty and territorial integrity of states" and calling for the withdrawal of the "U.S. armed invasion forces from Panama." Iraq's invasion of Kuwait was treated differently, in ways remote from the standard version, but readily discovered in print.

The inexpressible facts shed interesting light on the commentary of political analysts: Ronald Steel, for example, who muses today on the "conundrum" faced by the United States, which, "as the world's most powerful nation, faces greater constraints on its freedom to use force than does any other country." Hence Saddam's success in Kuwait as compared with Washington's inability to exert its will in Panama.

It is worth recalling that debate was effectively foreclosed in 1990-1991 as well. There was much discussion of whether sanctions would work, but none of whether they already had worked, perhaps shortly after Resolution 660 was passed. Fear that sanctions might have worked animated Washington's refusal to test Iraqi withdrawal offers from August 1990 to early January. With the rarest of exceptions, the information system kept tight discipline on the matter. Polls a few days before the January 1991 bombing showed 2-1 support for a peaceful settlement based on Iraqi withdrawal along with an international conference on the Israel-Arab conflict. Few among those who expressed this position could have heard any public advocacy of it; the media had loyally followed the President's lead, dismissing "linkage" as unthinkable—in this unique case. It is unlikely that any respondents knew that their views were shared by the Iraqi democratic opposition, barred from mainstream media. Or that an Iraqi proposal in the terms they advocated had been released a week earlier by U.S. officials who found it reasonable, and flatly rejected by Washington. Or that an Iraqi withdrawal offer had been considered by the National Security Council as early as mid-August, but dismissed, and effectively suppressed, apparently because it was feared that unmentioned Iraqi initiatives might "defuse the crisis," as the *New York Times* diplomatic correspondent obliquely reported Administration concerns.

Since then, Iraq has displaced Iran and Libya as the leading "rogue state." Others have never entered the ranks. Perhaps the most relevant case is Indonesia, which shifted from enemy to friend when General Suharto took power in 1965, presiding over an enormous slaughter that elicited great satisfaction in the West. Since then Suharto has been "our kind of guy," as the Clinton administration described him, while carrying out murderous aggression and endless atrocities against his own people; killing 10,000 Indonesians just in the 1980s, according to the personal testimony of "our guy," who wrote that "the corpses were left lying around as a form of shock therapy." In December 1975, the U.N. Security Council unanimously ordered Indonesia to withdraw its invading forces from East Timor "without delay" and called upon "all States to respect the territorial integrity of East Timor as well as the inalienable right of its people to self-determination." The United States responded by (secretly) increasing shipments of arms to the aggressors; Carter accelerated the arms flow once again as the attack reached near-genocidal levels in 1978. In his memoirs, U.N. Ambassador Daniel Patrick Moynihan takes pride in his success in rendering the United Nations "utterly ineffective in whatever measures it undertook," following the instructions of the State Department, which "wished things to turn out as they did and worked to bring this about." The United States also happily accepts the robbery of East Timor's oil (with participation of a U.S. company), in violation of any reasonable interpretation of international agreements.

The analogy to Iraq/Kuwait is close, though there are differences: to mention only the most obvious, U.S.-sponsored atrocities in East Timor were vastly beyond anything attributed to Saddam Hussein in Kuwait.

There are many other examples, though some of those commonly invoked should be treated with caution, particularly concerning Israel. The civilian toll of Israel's U.S.-backed invasion of Lebanon in 1982 exceeded Saddam's in Kuwait, and it remains in violation of a 1978 Security Council resolution ordering it to withdraw forthwith from Lebanon, along with numerous others regarding Jerusalem, the Golan Heights, and other matters; and there would be far more if the United States did not regularly veto such resolutions. But the common charge that Israel, particularly its current government, is violating U.N. 242 and the Oslo Accords, and that the United States exhibits a "double standard" by tolerating those violations, is dubious at best, based on serious misunderstanding of these agreements. From the outset, the Madrid-Oslo process was designed and implemented by U.S.-Israeli power to impose a Bantustan-style settlement. The Arab world has chosen to delude itself about the matter, as have many others, but they are clear in the actual documents, and particularly in the U.S.-supported projects of the Rabin-Peres governments, including those for which the current Likud government is now being denounced.

It is clearly untrue to claim that "Israel is not demonstrably in violation of Security Council decrees" (*New York Times*), but the reasons often given should be examined carefully.

Returning to Iraq, it surely qualifies as a leading criminal state. Defending the U.S. plan to attack Iraq at a televised public meeting on February 18, Secretaries Albright and Cohen repeatedly invoked the ultimate atrocity: Saddam was guilty of "using weapons of mass destruction against his neighbors as well as his own people," his most awesome crime. "It is very important for us to make clear that the United States and the civilized world cannot deal with somebody who is willing to use those weapons of mass destruction on his own people, not to speak of his neighbors," Albright emphasized in an angry response to a questioner who asked about U.S. support for Suharto. Shortly after, Senator Lott condemned Kofi Annan for seeking to cultivate a "human relationship with a mass murderer," and denounced the Administration for trusting a person who would sink so low.

Ringing words. Putting aside their evasion of the question raised, Albright and Cohen only forgot to mention—and commentators have been kind enough not to point out—that the acts that they now find so horrifying did not turn Iraq into a "rogue state." And Lott failed to note that his heroes Reagan and Bush forged unusually warm relations with the "mass murderer." There were no passionate calls for a military strike after Saddam's gassing of Kurds at Halabja in March 1988; on the contrary, the United States and Britain extended their strong support for the mass murderer, then also "our kind of guy." When ABC TV correspondent Charles Glass revealed the site of one of Saddam's biological warfare programs ten months after Halabja, the State Department denied the facts, and the story died; the Department "now issues briefings on the same site," Glass observes.

The two guardians of global order also expedited Saddam's other atrocities—including his use of cyanide, nerve gas, and other barbarous weapons—with intelligence, technology, and supplies, joining with many others. The Senate Banking Committee reported in 1994 that the U.S. Commerce Department had traced shipments of "biological materials" identical to those later found and destroyed by U.N. inspectors, Bill Blum recalls. These shipments continued at least until November 1989. A month later, Bush authorized new loans for his friend Saddam, to achieve the "goal of increasing U.S. exports and put us in a better position to deal with Iraq regarding its human rights record...," the State Department announced with a straight face, facing no criticism in the mainstream press (or even report).

Britain's record was exposed, at least in part, in an official inquiry (Scott Inquiry). The British government has just now been compelled to concede that it continued to grant licenses to British firms to export materials usable for biological weapons after the Scott report was published, at least until December 1996.

In a February 28 review of Western sales of materials usable for germ warfare and other weapons of mass destruction, the *Times* mentions one example of U.S. sales in the 1980s, including "deadly pathogens," with government approval, some from the Army's center for germ research in Fort Detrick. Just the tip of the iceberg, however.

A common current pretense is Saddam's crimes were unknown, so we are now properly shocked at the discovery and must "make clear" that we civilized folk "cannot deal with" the perpetrator of such crimes (Albright). The posture is cynical fraud. U.N. Reports of 1986 and 1987 condemned Iraq's use of chemical weapons. U.S. Embassy staffers in Turkey interviewed Kurdish survivors of chemical warfare attacks, and the CIA reported them to the State Department. Human Rights groups reported the atrocities at Halabja and elsewhere at once. Secretary of State George Shultz conceded that the United States had evidence on the matter. An investigative team sent by the Senate Foreign Relations Committee in 1988 found "overwhelming evidence of extensive use of chemical weapons against civilians," charging that Western acquiescence in Iraqi use of such weapons against Iran had emboldened Saddam to believe— correctly—that he could use them against his own people with impunity—actually against Kurds, hardly "the people" of this tribal-based thug. The chair of the Committee, Claiborne Pell, introduced the Prevention of Genocide Act of 1988, denouncing silence "while people are gassed" as "complicity," much as when "the world was silent as Hitler began a campaign that culminated in the near extermination of Europe's Jews," and warning that "we cannot be silent to genocide again." The Reagan administration strongly opposed sanctions and insisted that the matter be silenced, while extending its support for the mass murderer. In the Arab world, "the Kuwait press was amongst the most enthusiastic of the Arab media in supporting Baghdad's crusade against the Kurds," journalist Adel Darwish reports.

In January 1991, while the war drums were beating, the International Commission of Jurists observed to the U.N. Human Rights Commission that "After having perpetrated the most flagrant abuses on its own population without a word of reproach from the U.N., Iraq must have concluded it could do whatever it pleased"; United Nations in this context means the United States and Britain, primarily. That truth must be buried along with international law and other "utopian" distractions.

An unkind commentator might remark that recent U.S./U.K. toleration for poison gas and chemical warfare is not too surprising. The

British used chemical weapons in their 1919 intervention in North Russia against the Bolsheviks, with great success according to the British command. As Secretary of State at the War Office in 1919, Winston Churchill was enthusiastic about the prospects of "using poisoned gas against uncivilised tribes"—Kurds and Afghans—and authorized the RAF Middle East command to use chemical weapons "against recalcitrant Arabs as experiment," dismissing objections by the India office as "unreasonable" and deploring the "squeamishness about the use of gas": "we cannot in any circumstances acquiesce in the non-utilisation of any weapons which are available to procure a speedy termination of the disorder which prevails on the frontier," he explained; chemical weapons are merely "the application of Western science to modern warfare."

The Kennedy administration pioneered the massive use of chemical weapons against civilians as it launched its attack against South Vietnam in 1961-1962. There has been much rightful concern about the effects on U.S. soldiers, but not the incomparably worse effects on civilians. In an Israeli mass-circulation daily, the respected journalist Amnon Kapeliouk reported on his 1988 visit to Vietnam, where he found that "Thousands of Vietnamese still die from the effects of American chemical warfare," citing estimates of one-quarter of a million victims in South Vietnam and describing the "terrifying" scenes in hospitals in the south with children dying of cancer and hideous birth deformities. It was South Vietnam that was targeted for chemical warfare, not the North, where these consequences are not found, he reports. There is also substantial evidence of U.S. use of biological weapons against Cuba, reported as minor news in 1977, and at worst only a small component of continuing U.S. terror.

These precedents aside, the United States and Britain are now engaged in a deadly form of biological warfare in Iraq. The destruction of infrastructure and banning of imports to repair it has caused disease, malnutrition, and early death on a huge scale, including 567,000 children by 1995, according to U.N. investigations; UNICEF reports 4,500 children dying a month in 1996. In a bitter condemnation of the sanctions (January 20, 1998), 54 Catholic Bishops quoted the Archbishop of the southern region of Iraq, who reports that "epidemics rage, taking away infants and the sick by the thousands" while "those children who survive disease succumb to malnutrition." The Bishop's statement, reported in full in Stanley Heller's journal, *The Struggle*, received scant mention in the press. The United States and Britain have taken the lead in blocking aid programs—for example, delaying approval for ambulances on the grounds that they could be used to transport troops, barring insecticides to prevent

NOAM CHOMSKY

spread of disease and spare parts for sanitation systems. Meanwhile, western diplomats point out, "The U.S. had directly benefited from [the humanitarian] operation as much, if not more, than the Russians and the French," for example, by purchase of $600 million worth of Iraqi oil (second only to Russia) and sale by U.S. companies of $200 million in humanitarian goods to Iraq. They also report that most of the oil bought by Russian companies ends up in the United States.

Washington's support for Saddam reached such an extreme that it was even willing to overlook an Iraqi air force attack on the USS Stark, killing 37 of the crew, a privilege otherwise enjoyed only by Israel (in the case of the USS Liberty). It was Washington's decisive support for Saddam, well after the crimes that now so shock the Administration and Congress, that led to Iranian capitulation to "Baghdad and Washington," Dilip Hiro concludes in his history of the Iran-Iraq war. The two allies had "co-ordinate[d] their military operations against Teheran." The shooting down of an Iranian civilian airliner by the guided-missile cruiser Vincennes was the culmination of Washington's "diplomatic, military and economic campaign" in support of Saddam, he writes.

Saddam was also called upon to perform the usual services of a client state: for example, to train several hundred Libyans sent to Iraq by the United States so they could overthrow the

Qaddafi government, former Reagan White House aide Howard Teicher revealed.

It was not his massive crimes that elevated Saddam to the rank of "Beast of Baghdad." Rather, it was his stepping out of line, much as in the case of the far more minor criminal Noriega, whose major crimes were also committed while he was a U.S. client.

In passing, one might note that the destruction of Iran Air 655 in Iranian airspace by the Vincennes may come back to haunt Washington. The circumstances are suspicious, to say the least. In the Navy's official journal, Commander David Carlson wrote that he "wondered aloud in disbelief" as he observed from his nearby vessel as the Vincennes—then within Iranian territorial waters—shot down what was obviously a civilian airliner in a commercial corridor, perhaps out of "a need to prove the viability of Aegis," its high tech missile system. The commander and key officers "were rewarded with medals for their conduct," Marine Corps colonel (retired) David Evans observes in the same journal in an acid review of the Navy Department cover-up of the affair. President Bush informed the United Nations that "One thing is clear, and that is that the Vincennes acted in self-defense... in the midst of a naval attack initiated by Iranian vessels...," all lies Evans points out, though of no significance, given Bush's position that "I will never apologize for the United States of America—I don't care what the facts are." A retired Army colonel who attended the official hearings concluded that "our Navy is too dangerous to deploy."

It is difficult to avoid the thought that the destruction of Pan Am 103 over Lockerbie a few months later was Iranian retaliation, as stated explicitly by Iranian intelligence defector Abolhassem Mesbahi, also an aide to President Rafsanjani, "regarded as a credible and senior Iranian source in Germany and elsewhere," the *Guardian* reports. A 1991 U.S. intelligence document (National Security Agency), declassified in 1997, draws the same conclusion, alleging that Akbar Mohtashemi, a former Iranian interior minister, transferred $10 million "to bomb Pan Am 103 in retaliation for the U.S. shoot-down of the Iranian Airbus," referring to his connections with "the Al Abas and Abu Nidal terrorist groups." It is striking that despite the evidence and the clear motive, this is virtually the only act of terrorism not blamed on Iran. Rather, the United States and Britain have charged two Libyan nationals with the crime.

The charges against the Libyans have been widely disputed, including a detailed inquiry by Denis Phipps, former head of security at British Airways who served on the government's National Aviation Committee. The British organization of families of Lockerbie victims believe that there has been "a major cover-up" (spokesperson Dr. Jim Swire), and regard as more credible the account given in Alan Frankovich's documentary, *The Maltese Cross*, which provides evidence of the Iranian connection and a drug operation involving a courier working for the U.S. Drug Enforcement Administration. The film was shown at the British House of Commons and on British TV, but rejected here. The U.S. families keep strictly to Washington's version.

Also intriguing is the U.S./U.K. refusal to permit a trial of the accused Libyans. This takes the form of rejection of Libya's offer to release the accused for trial in some neutral venue: to a judge nominated by the U.N. (December 1991), a trial at the Hague "under Scottish law," etc. These proposals have been backed by the Arab League and the British relatives organization but flatly rejected by the United States and Britain. In March 1992, the U.N. Security Council passed a resolution imposing sanctions against Libya, with five absentions: China, Morocco (the only Arab member), India, Zimbabwe, Cape Verde. There was considerable arm-twisting: thus China was warned that it would lose U.S. trade preferences if it vetoed the resolution. The U.S. press has reported Libya's offer to release the suspects for trial, dismissing it as worthless and ridiculing Qaddafi's "dramatic gesture" of calling for the surrender of U.S. pilots who bombed two Libyan cities, killing 37 people, including his adopted daughter. Plainly, that is as absurd as requests by Cuba and Costa Rica for extradition of U.S. terrorists.

It is understandable that the United States and Britain should want to ensure a trial they can control, as in the case of the Noriega kidnapping. Any sensible defense lawyer would bring up the Iranian connection in a neutral venue. How long the charade can continue is unclear. In the midst of the current Iraq crisis, the World Court rejected the U.S./U.K. claim that it has no jurisdiction over the matter, and intends to launch a full hearing (13-2, with the U.S. and British judges opposed), which may make it harder to keep the lid on.

The Court ruling was welcomed by Libya and the British families. Washington and the U.S. media warned that the World Court ruling might prejudice the 1992 U.N. resolution that demanded that "Libya must surrender those accused of the Lockerbie bombing for trial in Scotland or the United States" (*New York Times*), that Libya "extradite the suspects to the United States and Britain" (AP). These claims are not accurate. The issue of transfer to Scotland or the United States never arose, and is not mentioned in the U.N. Resolutions. Resolution 731 (January 21, 1992) "Urges the Libyan Government immediately to provide a full and effective response" to requests "in connection with the legal procedures" related to attacks against Pan Am 103 and a French airliner.

Resolution 748 (March 31, 1992) "Decides that the Libyan Government must now comply without any further delay" with the request of Resolution 731, and that it renounce terrorism, calling for sanctions if Libya fails to do so. Resolution 731 was adopted in response to a U.S./U.K. declaration that Libya must "surrender for trial all those charged with the crime," with no further specification.

Press reports at the time were similarly inaccurate. Thus, reporting the U.S. dismissal of the Libyan offer to turn the suspects over to a neutral country, the *New York Times* highlighted the words: "Again, Libya tries to avoid a U.N. order." The *Washington Post* dismissed the offer as well, stating that "The Security Council contends that the suspects must be tried in U.S. or British courts." Doubtless Washington prefers to have matters seen in this light. A correct account was given in a 1992 opinion piece by international legal authority Alfred Rubin of the Fletcher School (*Christian Science Monitor*), who noted that the Security Council resolution makes no mention of extradition to the United States and Britain, and observes that its wording "departs so far from what the United States, Britain, and France are reported to have wanted that current public statements and press accounts reporting an American diplomatic triumph and U.N. pressures on Libya seem incomprehensible"; unfortunately, the performance is all too routine.

In the *New York Times*, British specialist on U.N. law Marc Weiler, in an op-ed, agreed with Rubin that the United States should follow the clear requirements of international law and accept Libya's proposal for World Court adjudication. Libya's response to the U.S./U.K. request was "precisely as mandated by international law," Weiler wrote, condemning the United States and Britain for having "flatly refused" to submit the issue to the World Court. Rubin and Weiler also ask obvious further questions: Suppose that New Zealand had resisted powerful French pressures to compel it to abandon its attempt to extradite the French government terrorists who had bombed the Rainbow Warrior in Auckland harbor? Or that Iran were to demand that the captain of the Vincennes be extradited? The World Court has now drawn the same conclusion as Rubin and Weiler.

The qualifications as "rogue state" are illuminated further by Washington's reaction to the uprisings in Iraq in March 1991, immediately after the cessation of hostilities. The State Department formally reiterated its refusal to have any dealings with the Iraqi democratic opposition, and as from before the Gulf War, they were virtually denied access to the major U.S. media. "Political meetings with them would not be appropriate for our policy at this time," State Department spokesperson Richard Boucher stated. "This time" happened to be March 14,

1991, while Saddam was decimating the south-ern opposition under the eyes of General Schwartzkopf, refusing even to permit rebelling military officers access to captured Iraqi arms. Had it not been for unexpected public reaction, Washington probably would not have extended even tepid support to rebelling Kurds, subjected to the same treatment shortly after.

Iraqi opposition leaders got the message. Leith Kubba, head of the London-based Iraqi Democratic Reform Movement, alleged that the United States favors a military dictatorship, insisting that "changes in the regime must come from within, from people already in power." London-based banker Ahmed Chalabi, head of the Iraqi National Congress, said that "the United States, covered by the fig leaf of non-interference in Iraqi affairs, is waiting for Saddam to butcher the insurgents in the hope that he can be overthrown later by a suitable officer," an attitude rooted in the U.S. policy of "supporting dictatorships to maintain stability."

Administration reasoning was outlined by *New York Times* chief diplomatic correspondent Thomas Friedman. While opposing a popular rebellion, Washington did hope that a military coup might remove Saddam, "and then Wash-ington would have the best of all worlds: an iron-fisted Iraqi junta without Saddam Hussein," a return to the days when Saddam's "iron fist... held Iraq together, much to the satisfaction of the

American allies Turkey and Saudi Arabia," not to speak of Washington. Two years later, in another useful recognition of reality, he observed that "it has always been American policy that the iron-fisted Mr. Hussein plays a useful role in holding Iraq together," maintaining "stability." There is little reason to believe that Washington has modified the preference for dictatorship over democracy deplored by the ignored Iraqi democratic opposition, though it doubtless would prefer a different "iron fist" at this point. If not, Saddam will have to do.

The concept "rogue state" is highly nuanced. Thus Cuba qualifies as a leading "rogue state" because of its alleged involvement in international terrorism, but the United States does not fall into the category despite its terrorist attacks against Cuba for close to 40 years, apparently continuing through last summer according to important investigative reporting of the *Miami Herald*, which failed to reach the national press (in the United States; it did in Europe). Cuba was a "rogue state" when its military forces were in Angola, backing the government against South African attacks supported by the United States. South Africa, in contrast, was not a rogue state then, nor during the Reagan years, when it caused over $60 billion in damage and 1.5 million deaths in neighboring states according to a U.N. commission, not to speak of some events at home—

and with ample U.S./U.K. support. The same exemption applies to Indonesia and many others.

The criteria are fairly clear: a "rogue state" is not simply a criminal state, but one that defies the orders of the powerful—who are, of course, exempt.

MORE ON "THE DEBATE"

That Saddam is a criminal is undoubtedly true, and one should be pleased, I suppose, that the United States and Britain, and mainstream doctrinal institutions, have at last joined those who "prematurely" condemned U.S./U.K. support for the mass murderer. It is also true that he poses a threat to anyone within his reach. On the comparison of the threat with others, there is little unanimity outside the United States and Britain, after their (ambiguous) transformation from August 1990. Their 1998 plan to use force was justified in terms of Saddam's threat to the region, but there was no way to conceal the fact that the people of the region objected to their salvation, so strenuously that governments were compelled to join in opposition.

Bahrein refused to allow U.S./British forces to use bases there. The president of the United Arab Emirates described U.S. threats of military action as "bad and loathsome," and declared that Iraq does not pose a threat to its neighbors. Saudi Defense Minister Prince Sultan had already stated that "We'll not agree and we are against striking

Iraq as a people and as a nation," causing Washington to refrain from a request to use Saudi bases. After Annan's mission, long-serving Saudi foreign minister Prince Saud al-Faisal reaffirmed that any use of Saudi air bases "has to be a U.N., not a U.S. issue."

An editorial in Egypt's quasi-official journal, *Al Ahram*, described Washington's stand as "coercive, aggressive, unwise and uncaring about the lives of Iraqis, who are unnecessarily subjected to sanctions and humiliation," and denounced the planned U.S. "aggression against Iraq." Jordan's Parliament condemned "any aggression against Iraq's territory and any harm that might come to the Iraqi people"; the Jordanian army was forced to seal off the city of Maan after two days of pro-Iraq rioting. A political science professor at Kuwait University warned that "Saddam has come to represent the voice of the voiceless in the Arab world," expressing popular frustration over the "New World Order" and Washington's advocacy of Israeli interests.

Even in Kuwait, support for the U.S. stance was at best "tepid" and "cynical over U.S. motives," the press recognized. "Voices in the streets of the Arab world, from Cairo's teeming slums to the Arabian Peninsula's shiny capitals, have been rising in anger as the American drumbeat of war against Iraq grows louder," *Boston Globe* correspondent Charles Sennott reported.

The Iraqi democratic opposition was granted a slight exposure in the mainstream, breaking the previous pattern. In a telephone interview with the *New York Times*, Ahmed Chalabi reiterated the position that had been reported in greater detail in London weeks earlier: "Without a political plan to remove Saddam's regime, military strikes will be counter-productive," he argued, killing thousands of Iraqis, leaving Saddam perhaps even strengthened along with his weapons of mass destruction and with "an excuse to throw out UNSCOM [the U.N. inspectors]," who have in fact destroyed vastly more weapons and production facilities than the 1991 bombing. U.S./U.K. plans would "be worse than nothing." Interviews with opposition leaders from several groups found "near unanimity" in opposing military action that did not lay the basis for an uprising to overthrow Saddam. Speaking to a Parliamentary committee, Chalabi held that it was "morally indefensible to strike Iraq without a strategy" for removing Saddam.

In London, the opposition also outlined an alternative program: (1) declare Saddam a war criminal; (2) recognize a provisional Iraqi government formed by the opposition; (3) unfreeze hundreds of millions of dollars of Iraqi assets abroad; restrict Saddam's forces by a "no-drive zone" or extend the "no-flight zone" to cover the whole country. The United States should "help the Iraqi people remove Saddam from power," Chalabi told the Senate Armed Services Committee. Along with other opposition leaders, he "rejected assassination, covert U.S. operations or U.S. ground troops," Reuters reported, calling instead for "a popular insurgency." Similar proposals have occasionally appeared in the United States. Washington claims to have attempted support for opposition groups, but their own interpretation is different. Chalabi's view, published in England, is much as it was years earlier: "everyone says Saddam is boxed in, but it is the Americans and British who are boxed in by their refusal to support the idea of political change."

Regional opposition was regarded as a problem to be evaded, not a factor to be taken into account, any more than international law. The same was true of warnings by senior U.N. and other international relief officials in Iraq that the planned bombing might have a "catastrophic" effect on people already suffering miserably, and might terminate the humanitarian operations that have brought at least some relief. What matters is to establish that "What We Say Goes," as President Bush triumphantly proclaimed, announcing the New World Order as bombs and missiles were falling in 1991.

As Kofi Annan was preparing to go to Baghdad, former Iranian president Rafsanjani, "still a pivotal figure in Tehran, was given an audience by the ailing King Fahd in Saudi Arabia," British Middle East correspondent David Gardner reported, "in contrast to the treatment experienced by Madeleine Albright... on her recent trips to Riyadh seeking support from America's main Gulf ally." As Rafsanjani's ten-day visit ended on March 2, foreign minister Prince Saud described it as "one more step in the right direction towards improving relations," reiterating that "the greatest destabilising element in the Middle East and the cause of all other problems in the region" is Israel's policy towards the Palestinians and U.S. support for it, which might activate popular forces that Saudi Arabia greatly fears, as well as undermining its legitimacy as "guardian" of Islamic holy places, including the Dome of the Rock in East Jerusalem, now effectively annexed by U.S./Israeli programs as part of their intent to extend "greater Jerusalem" virtually to the Jordan Valley, to be retained by Israel. Shortly before, the Arab states had boycotted a U.S.-sponsored economic summit in Qatar that was intended to advance the "New Middle East" project of Clinton and Peres. Instead, they attended an Islamic conference in Teheran in December, joined even by Iraq.

These are tendencies of considerable import, relating to the background concerns that motivate U.S. policy in the region: its insistence, since World War II, on controlling the world's major energy reserves. As many have observed, in the Arab world there is growing fear and resentment of the long-standing Israel-Turkey alliance that was formalized in 1996, now greatly strengthened. For some years, it had been a component of the U.S. strategy of controlling the region with "local cops on the beat," as Nixon's Defense Secretary put the matter. There is apparently a growing appreciation of the Iranian advocacy of regional security arrangements to replace U.S. domination. A related matter is the intensifying conflict over pipelines to bring Central Asian oil to the rich countries, one natural outlet being via Iran.

And U.S. energy corporations will not be happy to see foreign rivals—now including China and Russia as well—gain privileged access to Iraqi oil reserves, second only to Saudi Arabia in scale, or to Iran's natural gas, oil, and other resources.

For the present, Clinton planners may well be relieved to have escaped temporarily from the "box" they had constructed that was leaving them no option but a bombing of Iraq that could have been harmful even to the interests they represent. The respite is temporary. It offers opportunities to citizens of the warrior states to bring about changes of consciousness and commitment that could make a great difference in the not too distant future.

ON THE FIFTIETH ANNIVERSARY OF THE UNIVERSAL DECLARATION OF HUMAN RIGHTS

by Ramsey Clark

"The world has never had a good definition of the word liberty, and the American people, just now, are much in want of one. We all declare for liberty, but in using the same word we do not all mean the same thing." So observed Abraham Lincoln at, for him, the darkest moment of the American Civil War. He had just received reports of the massacre of 800 Union soldiers, former slaves whose ancestors were brought from Africa in chains. They were the first such unit to be engaged in combat. Caught and overwhelmed at Ft. Pillow, Tennessee on the Mississippi river by a much larger Confederate cavalry force under Nathan Bedford Forrest, every man was killed. Forrest reported the river ran red for hundreds of yards. After the war Forrest was a founder of the Ku Klux Klan and engaged in racist violence for two decades.

Four score and four years after the Ft. Pillow massacre, in the Preamble to the Universal Declaration of Human Rights on December 10, 1948, the U.N. General Assembly found "a common understanding of these rights and freedoms is of the greatest importance," and proclaimed its declaration in order to provide "a good definition."

The Universal Declaration was dominated by the experience, concerns, interests and values of a narrow segment of the "people of the United Nations," primarily the governments of the rich nations, primarily the United States, England and France. It emphasized political rights developed over centuries from their histories with little concern for economic, social and cultural rights. Still it was and remains an important contribution in the continuing struggle for justice.

In the fifth paragraph of its preamble the Declaration notes the United Nations has affirmed "... the dignity and worth of the human person and the equal rights of men and women and have determined to promote social progress and better standards of life in larger freedom." Article 1 provides "All human beings are born free and equal in dignity and rights." Article 5 states, "No one shall be subjected to torture or to cruel, inhuman or degrading treatment or punishment." Article 25 declares, "(1)Everyone has the right to a standard of living adequate for the health and well-being of himself and of his family, including food, clothing, housing and medical care..."

The United States government pays lip service to the Declaration, but its courts have consistently refused to enforce its provisions reasoning it is not a legally binding treaty, or contract, but only a declaration. This ignores the fact that international law recognizes the provisions of the Declaration as being incorporated into customary international law which is binding on all nations.

The most fundamental, dangerous and harmful violation of the Universal Declaration of Human Rights on its fifteenth birthday is economic sanctions imposed on entire populations. The United States alone blockades eleven million Cubans in the face of the most recent General Assembly resolution approved by 157 nations condemning the blockade, with only the United States and Israel in opposition. The entire population of Cuba and every Cuban has had the "right to a standard of living adequate for health and well being... including food, clothing, housing and medical care" deliberately violated by the United States blockade.

Security Council sanctions against Iraq, which are forced by the United States, have devastated the entire nation, taking the lives of more than 1,500,000 people, mostly infants, children, chronically ill and elderly, and harming millions more by hunger, sickness and sorrow. The sanctions destroy the "dignity and rights" of the people of Iraq and are the most extreme form of "cruel, inhuman and degrading treatment," which are prohibited by the Declaration.

Despite the cruelest destruction of the most basic human rights and liberties of all the people in Iraq, including rights to medicine, safe drinking water and sufficient food, the United States government, with the major mass media in near perfect harmony, proclaims itself the world's champion of liberty and human rights. The problem as Lincoln surely knew is not merely one of definitions. It is a problem of power, will and accountability. The United States intends to have its way and serve its own interests, with Iraq, Cuba, Libya, Iran, the Sudan and many other countries whatever the consequences to the liberties and rights of those who live there.

The United States control over and its concerted action with the mass media enables it to demonize such countries, its victims, for "terrorism, "threats to world peace and human rights violations at the very time it rains Tomahawk cruise missiles on them and motivates and finances armed insurrections and violence against them. At the same time the United States increases its own staggeringly large prison industry, with more than a million persons confined, including 40 percent of all African-American males between 17 and 27 years old in the State of California. Simultaneously the United States spends more on its military than the ten largest military budgets of other nations combined, sells most of the arms and sophisticated weapons still increasing worldwide while rejecting an international convention to prohibit land mines and an international court of criminal justice. And the United States maintains and deploys the great majority of all weapons of mass destruction existent on earth, nuclear, chemical, biological and the most deadly of all— economic sanctions.

It is imperative that clear definitions of all fundamental rights of people, be clearly inscribed in international law, including economic rights which are most basic to human need and on which all other rights are dependent and rights to freedom from military aggression by a superpower or its surrogates.

But without a passionate commitment by the people of the United States and other major powers to stop their own governments from violating those definitions of human rights, hold them accountable for their acts and to prevent their own media from seducing them into acceptance or complacency, there will be no protection for the poor and powerless and no correspondence between the words of rich and powerful nations and their deeds.

We can be thankful for the Universal Declaration of Human Rights, but together the people of the world must do better to define and protect the humanity of the people.

EDWARD W. SAID was born in Jerusalem, Palestine and attended schools there and in Cairo, Egypt. He is Old Dominion Foundation Professor in the Humanities at Columbia University. He is the author of *Orientalism*, *Covering Islam*, *After the Last Sky*, *Culture and Imperialism*, and many others. He was formerly a member of the Palestine National Council.

NOAM CHOMSKY is an activist, writer, and professor of linguistics at Massachusetts Institute of Technology, where he has taught since 1955. His most recent book is *Profit Over People: Neoliberalism and Global Order* (Seven Stories Press, 1998). Chomsky has published many titles in the Open Media Pamphlet Series, including *Media Control: The Spectacular Achievements of Propaganda*.

RAMSEY CLARK is an attorney, teacher, and writer. He served as Attorney General of the United States during the Johnson Administration. He is actively engaged in practice of law in fields of law, peace, disarmament, human rights, civil rights, civil liberties, voting rights, health, education and others. In 1991 he founded the International Action Center .

ACTIVIST RESOURCES

Z NET
Z magazine's excellent web site posts activist alerts, progressive analysis, and hosts a variety of discussion areas on politics and social change.
www.zmag.org/znettopnoanimation.html

INTERNATIONAL ACTION CENTER
Founded by former Attorney General Ramsey Clark in 1991, this activist organization coordinates protests of U.S. military aggression and foreign policy.
39 West 14th Street
Room 206
New York, NY 10011
Tel: 212. 633. 6646
Fax: 212. 633. 2889
email: iacenter@iacenter.org

VOICES IN THE WILDERNESS
1460 West Carmen Ave.
Chicago, IL 60640
tel: 773. 784. 8065
fax: 773. 784. 8837
email: kkelly@igc.apc.org
www.nonviolence.org/vitw/

PEACE ACTION
475 Riverside Drive, #242
New York, NY 10415
tel:212. 870. 2304
fax: 212. 870. 2243
email: metropeace@aol.com

MUSLIM PEACE FELLOWSHIP
PO Box 271
Nyack, NY 10960
tel: 914. 358. 4601
fax: 914. 358. 4924
email: mpf@igc.apc.org
www.nonviolence.org

STUDENT COALTION FOR PEACE
WITH THE IRAQI PEOPLE
1164 Templeton Place
St. Louis, MO 63017
tel: 314. 434. 3473
fax: 314. 434. 6146
email: peaceiraq@aol.com